~ HUDDLE ~
PARTICIPANT GUIDE

S0-BSY-822

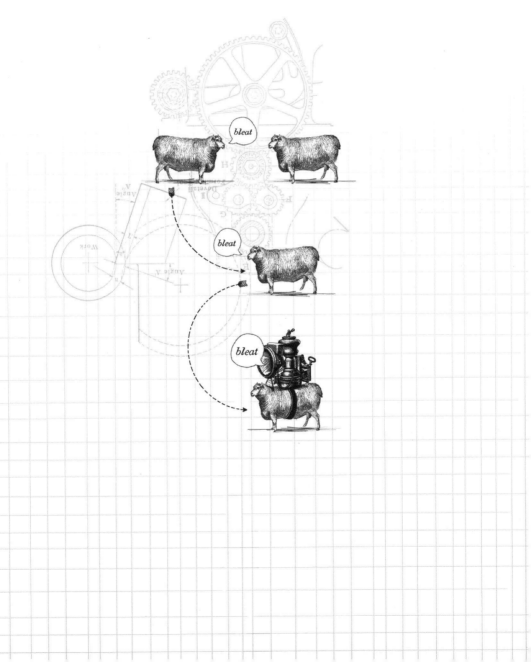

HUDDLE PARTICIPANT GUIDE
© Copyright 2012 by Mike Breen

All rights reserved. No part of this book may be reproduced,
stored in a retrieval system, or transmitted in any form or by
any means, electronic, mechanical, photocopying, recording or
otherwise, without the written prior permission of the authors
and copyright owner, or a licence permitting restricted copying,
except for brief quotations in books and critical reviews.
For information, write to 3 Dimension Ministries, PO Box 719,
Pawleys Island, SC 29585, USA or www.weare3dm.com

All Scripture quotations, unless otherwise noted, are taken from
the Holy Bible, New International Version® (NIV). Copyright
© 1973, 1978, 1984 by International Bible Society. Used by
permission of Zondervan Publishing House. All rights reserved.

First printing 2012
Printed in China
4 5 6 7 8 9 10 11 12 13 Printing/Year 15 14 13 12 11 10

Cover Design: Blake Berg
Editor/Interior Design: Pete Berg
ISBN: 978-0-9846643-4-4

TABLE OF CONTENTS

～ HUDDLE ～ CONTACT INFO

Leader ....

Phone .... Email ....

Huddle Members

Name ....

Phone .... Email ....

Name ....

Phone .... Email ....

Name ....

Phone .... Email ....

Name ....

Phone .... Email ....

Name ....

Phone .... Email ....

Name ....

Phone .... Email ....

∾ WHAT IS ∾ A HUDDLE?

A Huddle is a discipleship vehicle for current or future leaders that provides support, challenge, training, and accountability and is led by a discipling leader. Typically, Huddles have 4-8 people in them and the participants are invited into a discipling relationship by the Huddle leader.

The purpose of Huddle is to provide a regular and rhythmic time for this group of current or future leaders to be invested in, discipled and trained so they can then go and do the same for others. People in a Huddle are expected, at some point in the journey, to lead a group of their own and build a discipling culture within it. That might mean starting a Huddle of their own, or it could mean leading a small group or another discipleship vehicle.

There are a few things that uniquely characterize Huddle:

1. **Two questions.** At the conclusion of each Huddle, each participant will be able to answer these two questions: What is God saying to me and what am I going to do about it? These are the two fundamental questions of Christian spirituality as Jesus lays out in the Parable of the Wise and Foolish Man at the end of the Sermon on the Mount.

2. **Accountability.** At the beginning of the next Huddle, each participant will be asked how their plan went. Rather than a view of accountability that looks like spiritual policing, Huddle is a place of spiritual partnership.

3. **Language.** A place where the group will learn a common discipling language that will not only shape their life, but that they can also pass on to others.

4. **Leader.** A Huddle is not a place where the leader is acting like a facilitator, but is taking the group on a specific journey together. The leader is offering their life as something to be examined for how Jesus is actively working in it. They are certainly not a perfect example, but they can serve as a living one.

5. **Reproduction.** An expectation that at some point, each participant will begin leading a discipling vehicle of their own.

This is just a snapshot of Huddle. We could spend much time and ink explaining Huddle, but as with many things, it's simply better to experience it. If you do have more questions, we encourage you to bring your questions to your Huddle leader.

COACHING TIP

Things you'll need for Huddle each week:

1) A copy of the book Building a Discipling Culture

2) This Huddle Participant Guide

✑ IT'S ORGANIZED ✑ AND ORGANIC

Huddle is the ongoing, intentional, structured investment into the lives of future or current leaders where they are learning to listen and respond to the voice of God. A leader invests his or her life into the lives of others, encouraging them to step more and more into the Kingdom and live accountable lives.

However, the call to discipleship is an invitation into the life of the Huddle leader, not just Huddle experience. It is both an organized and organic expression of relationship. The vehicle of HUDDLE is on the organized spectrum; however, it is crucial we realize the organic component best described as ACCESS to the life of the Huddle leader. In other words, you'll be spending more time with them and receive additional investment from them outside of only a 90-minute window of time when Huddle happens.

This is an extraordinary opportunity, as the Huddle leader is not simply committing to one space and place of time each week. Rather, they are offering an invitation into their life, alongside Huddle, so you will truly receive the investment needed for a discipling relationship.

Discipleship is...

ORGANIZED / STRUCTURED	ORGANIC / SPONTANEOUS

◄ – ►

Huddle   *Access to leader's life*

✑ GENERAL ✑ GUIDELINES

Make it a priority. You need to invest the time to receive the most out of it. You'll need to be at every Huddle save out-of-the-blue situations.

Choose to be vulnerable. This is absolutely crucial — you need to choose to let your barriers down and be open. You may be tempted to be guarded for a number of months, but this completely misses the point of Huddle and is not fair to the other members of the group who are allowing themselves to be genuinely accountable.

Treat others with respect. This helps achieve and maintain the openness just spoken of. Not just the leader, but every individual member helps create a safe and secure environment for that group.

Have fun. Laugh a lot! Sometimes we forget that Jesus seemed to have a particularly good sense of humor. The general rule is that your times together will be relaxed but focused. Yes, of course there will be serious and profound moments, but you also want to come from Huddle feeling refreshed and invigorated. Laughing with friends in a safe environment is a great way to achieve that.

Give as well as receive. Huddle is not a consumer product. You need to come prepared to give of yourself both as you share your story, and as you help challenge and affirm others.

Commitment to the leader. For whatever reason, God has put this person in your life and in a Huddle they are leading. Commit to trusting this and where God is taking you. There is no question that your leader has flaws that you will quickly see, but God's grace can be more evident in those.

Build relationships. Some of the other people in your Huddle you may know well, others less so or not at all. While the commitment is to the leader and the gatherings they call, nevertheless it can be a much fuller experience if you spend time with other people in the Huddle.

～ WHAT ARE ～ LIFESHAPES?

Most Christians we've met have the ability to invest in the people God has put around them but usually don't for three basic reasons:

1. They aren't sure how to disciple people well. And so rather than screw it up, they decide not to.

2. They don't know where to begin. "What is most important for people to know? How can I make sure it's not just information in their head but they live it out as well?"

3. They don't have a discipling language that the people they are investing in will be able to easily remember.

What LifeShapes does is take many of the essential teachings and principles of the Bible and Jesus and gives people an easy way to remember each key concept: A shape. The point isn't just that you would learn it so that it shapes your life (though that's incredibly important); but it's just as important that you are able to remember it so you can share it with other people as you are investing in them. The shapes are simply a memory tool.

The shapes aren't the point. The point is scripture and making sure that the reality of scripture is sinking down into every part and practice of our being.

～ LIVING A ～ MISSIONAL LIFE

Discipleship is learning to be and to do all the things that Jesus could do. One man put it this way: *A disciple is who Jesus would be if he were you.*

And one of the key things Jesus did, taught his disciples to do and we see every-which-way in the early church, is living a life that is constantly inviting people into the Kingdom of God. Jesus wanted people to know his Father and know the goodness of his coming Kingdom. Sometimes that's by the way we act in any given circumstance. Sometimes it's by what we say and how we proclaim the Gospel.

Here's what we can say: If Jesus were you, he'd be inviting people into the Kingdom of which he is King! So if we are going to be learners of Jesus and teach others to be the same, we need to embrace the same missional lifestyle we see in the Bible. Being a disciple of Jesus is the opportunity of a lifetime and we want the whole world to have that opportunity.

Because of that, your Huddle won't only be times with your group talking about What God is saying to you and what you're doing to do about. There will be regular times when you go out together as a group to learn how to do this well. Unfortunately, many of us have a pretty unhelpful understanding of "evangelism." In fact, we've been taught to do things that Jesus purposefully didn't teach his disciples and we don't see in the early church and it's left a bad taste in our mouths or perhaps made us afraid of ever engaging.

Rather, the picture that Jesus gives is actually invigorating, fun, and, when you learn how to do it, is actually pretty easy. The times when the Huddle learns to engage with Jesus' "Person of Peace" strategy together will prove to be some of the most important moments for your Huddle.

∽ SHAPE ∽
KEY

Invitation + Challenge Matrix:
Invitation and Challenge

Circle:
Spiritual Breakthrough

Covenant + Kingdom:
Scripture Defining Reality

Semi-circle:
Rhythms of Life

Triangle:
Balanced and Deep Relationships

Square:
Multiplying Missional Disciples

Pentagon:
Personal Calling

Hexagon:
Prayer

Heptagon:
Communal Spiritual Health

Octagon:
Relational Mission

Invitation + Challenge:

Key Scripture: Matthew 16:13-24

....
....
....
....
....
....
....
....
....

Date ....

What is God saying to me?

....
....

What am I going to do about it?

....
....
....

Date ....

What is God saying to me?

....
....

What am I going to do about it?

....
....
....

Spiritual Breakthrough:

Key Scriptures:
- *Mark 1:14-15*
- *Matthew 7:24-29*

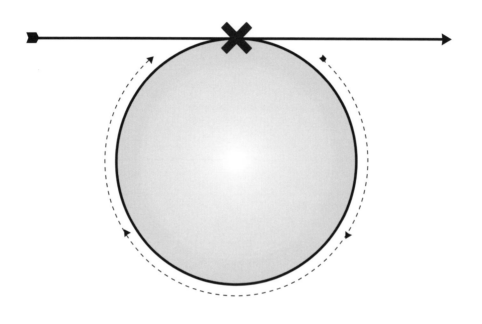

....
....
....
....
....
....
....

....
....
....
....
....
....
....
....
....
....

Date ....

What is God saying to me?

....
....

What am I going to do about it?

....
....
....

Date ....

What is God saying to me?

....
....

What am I going to do about it?

....
....
....

Scripture Defining Reality:

Key Scripture: Genesis 1:26-28

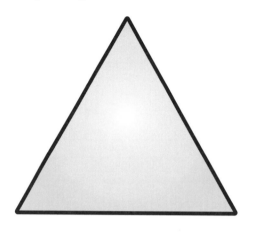

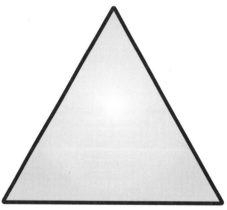

....
....
....
....
....
....
....
....

Date ....

What is God saying to me?

....
....

What am I going to do about it?

....
....
....

Date ....

What is God saying to me?

....
....

What am I going to do about it?

....
....
....

Rhythms of Life:

Key Scripture: John 15:1-12

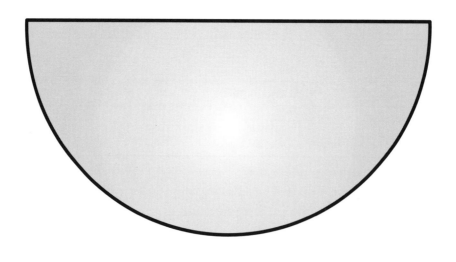

....

....

....

....

....

....

....

....

....

Date ....

What is God saying to me?

....

....

What am I going to do about it?

....

....

....

Date ....

What is God saying to me?

....

....

What am I going to do about it?

....

....

....

Balanced and Deep Relationships:

Key Scripture: Mark 9:2-29

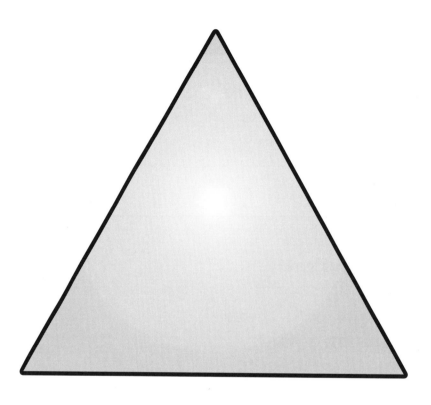

....

....

....

....

....

....

....

....

....
....
....
....
....
....
....
....
....

Date ....

What is God saying to me?

....
....

What am I going to do about it?

....
....
....

Date ....

What is God saying to me?

....
....

What am I going to do about it?

....
....
....

Multiplying Missional Disciples:

Key Scriptures:

- *Matthew 4:18-22*
- *Luke 12:22-32*
- *Mark 9:14-29*
- *John 20:19-23*

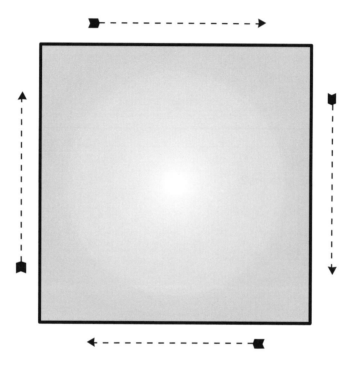

....
....
....
....
....
....
....
....

....

....

....

....

....

....

....

....

....

Date ....

What is God saying to me?

....

....

What am I going to do about it?

....

....

....

Date ....

What is God saying to me?

....

....

What am I going to do about it?

....

....

....

Personal Calling:

Key Scripture: Ephesians 4:11-14

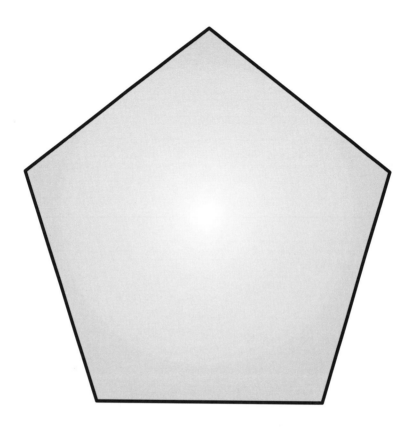

....
....
....
....
....
....
....
....

....
....
....
....
....
....
....
....
....

Date ....

What is God saying to me?

....

....

What am I going to do about it?

....

....

....

Date ....

What is God saying to me?

....

....

What am I going to do about it?

....

....

....

Prayer:

Key Scripture: Matthew 6:9-13

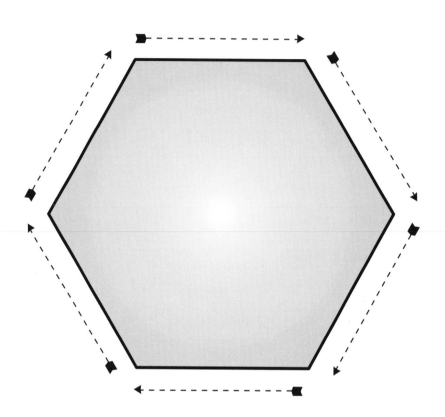

....
....
....
....
....
....
....
....
....

Date ....

What is God saying to me?

....
....

What am I going to do about it?

....
....
....

Date ....

What is God saying to me?

....
....

What am I going to do about it?

....
....
....

Communal Spiritual Health:

Key Scripture: Romans 12:4-5

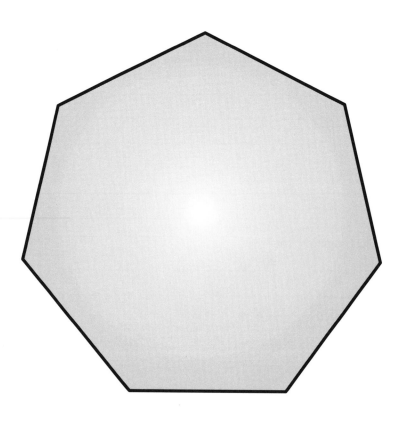

....

....

....

....

....

....

....

....

Date ....

What is God saying to me?

....

....

What am I going to do about it?

....

....

....

Date ....

What is God saying to me?

....

....

What am I going to do about it?

....

....

....

Relational Mission:

Key Scripture: Luke 10:1-16

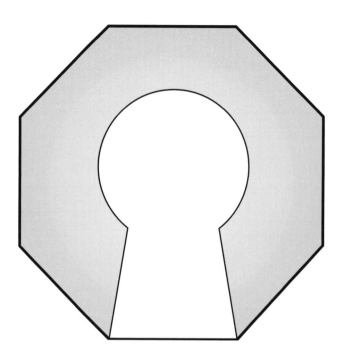

....

....

....

....

....

....

....

....

....
....
....
....
....
....
....
....

Date ....

What is God saying to me?

....

What am I going to do about it?

....
....
....

Date ....

What is God saying to me?

....

What am I going to do about it?

....
....
....

APPENDIX

∿ CHARACTER ∿ QUESTIONS

UP

Do I make enough space for prayer?

Do I pursue intimacy with Jesus?

What is on my heart for intercession?

Am I living in the power of the Spirit?

Am I seeing personal revival?

Do I still feel pleasure?

Am I living in a state of peace?

Am I afraid or nervous?

Am I obedient to God's prompting?

IN

Do I love the flock?

Is time a blessing or a curse?

Am I resting enough?

How are my relationships with my friends?

Am I experiencing intimacy in relationships?

Do I keep my promises?

How easy is it for me to trust people?

Am I discipling others?

Is my family happy?

Am I sleeping/eating well?

Am I making myself vulnerable to others?

OUT

Do I have a heart for the lost?

How often do I share my faith?

Do I leave time for relationships with non-Christians?

Am I running the race with perseverance?

Do I have a vision?

Am I looking after the least of these? (the poor, vulnerable, forgotten)

Am I dying to success?

Am I proud or ashamed of the Gospel?

Am I a servant?

Do I find it easy to recognize people of peace?

Can I take risks?

∾ SKILLS ∾ QUESTIONS

UP

Is the worship in my group dynamic and full of intimacy?

Do I find it easy to receive guidance for the next step in the life of my group?

How easy is it to talk to a whole group "from the front"?

Can I teach effectively from God's word?

Does my group share the vision God has given me?

Do I feel relaxed about leading times of Holy Spirit ministry?

IN

Do members of my group feel cared for?

Am I effective at resolving conflict?

Do I take on the discipline of confrontation?

Have I defined my own boundaries well?

Am I flexible?

How are my weaknesses as a leader compensated for by others?

How do I cope with over-dependent people?

How do I cope with controlling group members?

Are there difficulties in my relationships with co-leaders/assistant leaders?

OUT

Is my group growing?

Am I too controlling as a leader?

How welcoming is my group to new people?

Can all group members identify at least one Person of Peace?

Am I using leaders in my group effectively?

Do I find it easy to multiply groups?

Are those I am discipling turning into effective leaders?

Is my group effective in regularly doing OUT activity?

Does my group have a single people group in mind?

～ COVENANT ～
AND KINGDOM

The following is a excerpt from Mike Breen's book, *Covenant and Kingdom: The DNA of the Bible*. This will briefly outline the main concepts explored in understanding these two themes of scripture. For a much greater look into these ideas, feel free to pick up the book, available in paperback or ebook.

As Jesus reveals his relationship with his heavenly Father, Jesus invites us into a new depth of understanding of the Covenant. He offers to us the relationship that he enjoys with the Father.

FATHER

John's gospel—the gospel of the Covenant—defines the relationship that exists between God the Father and the Son. The Son is revealed as Jesus throughout the gospel.

Jesus says that he does only what he sees the Father doing (John 5:19). In shared identity, common purpose is forged. As his disciples mature in their relationship with him, Jesus reveals that they will share in a common relationship with the one that he calls Father and that together they will fashion the cords that will hold the Covenant together:

> "If anyone loves me, he will obey my teaching. My Father will love him, and we will come to him and make our home with him." (John 14:23)

Jesus came as one who was and is in radical, deep and intimate Covenant with the God of heaven. Today, he draws people to himself and builds a community of people who follow him, who want to become more like him and enter more into the realities of the Covenant that Jesus shares with his Father.

IDENTITY

Identity flows from the one who gives us life. We are children of God, born again into a new family, given a new name and a new identity by which we can gain access to all of the resources of our Covenant partner.

The New Testament teaches that when we are baptized we embrace our new identity. Jesus connects us to God and defines who we are. We bear his Name, and everything he has is ours. Our identity is so caught up with God's that the New Testament is able to say that we are heirs of heaven and co-heirs with Christ. God's commitment to us is written indelibly in the blood of Jesus. As we share in the Covenant meal that Jesus gave, the bread and wine help us to remember who he is and who we are.

OBEDIENCE

The New Covenant means that God's code of behavior for his people—"the Law"—is now written in our hearts. This happens when the Holy Spirit fills us and gives us new life when we are born again as God's children. Now we are free to obey God because this is truly a reflection of who we are. We choose to obey because this is the most consistent way of expressing our identity. What we do tells the world who we are:

> "If you love me, you will obey what I command." (John 14:15)

Obedience is always an act of love. Because of our shared Covenant identity with Jesus, we do the things he did:

> "I tell you the truth, anyone who has faith in me will do what I have been doing. He will do even greater things than these, because I am going to the Father." (John 14:12)

Exercising this life of Covenant oneness means living a life of security and confidence:

"And I will do whatever you ask in my name, so that the Son may bring glory to the Father. You may ask me for anything in my name, and I will do it." (John 14:13-14)

It may be helpful to sum this up visually in the same way that we did in the Old Testament Summary:

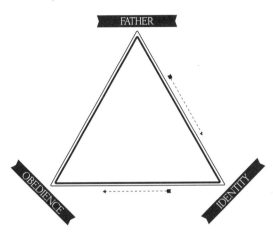

The Covenant begins with the Father, who gives us our identity. Now we are able to obey because as children of God we are empowered to do so. At times, we may find ourselves seeking to approach God through obedience rather than in simple recognition of our identity. When we do this, we fall into the trap of the Pharisees whom Jesus encountered. As we are God's children, he is already pleased with us, and this knowledge liberates us from the legalistic observance that so often leads to frustration and guilt.

SUMMARY OF KINGDOM IN THE NEW TESTAMENT

It is not with a show of majestic judgment that Jesus revealed the Kingship of God. Rather, it was with servant-hearted tenderness toward us, his wayward subjects. His sacrificial love brought the ultimate victory of the Kingdom over our enemies of sin, death and hell.

Until the birth of Jesus, the prophets foresaw only the coming of the King. But now the King has come among us. The King of heaven has taken on flesh and has chosen to walk among his wayward subjects, to reveal the future he has prepared for us, a future that we can taste now if only we will surrender to his Kingship.

In almost every expression of earthly kingdom, the monarch benefits most from its existence. With the Kingdom of heaven, however, the Kingdom is for the subjects. The King is a servant King who wants his people to be the greatest recipients of its benefits. In response to receiving all the blessings, the people of the King offer him their love and loyalty, glory and honor.

Again the Kingdom (or Kingship) of God is expressed in three key words: King, authority and power.

KING

As the servant King, Jesus constantly offered himself as the doorway to the future Kingdom. He looked for those who needed forgiveness; he searched for those who needed restoration or healing. Jesus the King was single-minded in his determination to reveal his Kingship. He sought the lost, fed the hungry, mended the broken and healed the sick. He told stories, painting pictures of a life worth living and a future worth dying for.

Usually the King's glory was veiled, but occasionally he was seen in all his splendor: at his baptism when heaven stood open, on the Mount of Transfiguration with the enveloping cloud of glory and in the Ascension when he made the return journey to the heavenly Kingdom.

AUTHORITY

The Kingdom is all about the King and his Kingship. But this King is completely committed to his subjects, desiring that they might fully reflect him as they represent him, doing all that he did and living as he lived.

Authority simply means the qualification to act. In the gospels, we read of Jesus' amazing authority as he represented God's Kingship. In turn, having followed him and learnt to imitate his life, his disciples chose to receive his authorization to act on his behalf. In the same way, we are commissioned to act on his behalf. Disciples choose to give as they have received—giving forgiveness, healing, deliverance and blessing.

POWER

In the United States and some other countries, police officers acting on behalf of their commissioning government are given two vital symbols of office—a badge to identify who they are and a gun that enables them to carry out their job. We need to carry the badge and the gun. If authority is our badge of office, then power is our gun with which we are equipped to take on the task.

Similar to Jesus, our power comes from the presence of the Holy Spirit. The Spirit of God himself connects us to the Kingdom for which we long. It is by him that we "taste the powers of the coming age" (Hebrews 6:4-5).

As with the Old Testament Summary, it may be helpful to portray graphically the connection of these three vital elements. The Kingdom begins with the King, who exercises authority through us his representatives, and with that authority, he sends power for us to be able to do all that he wants us to do:

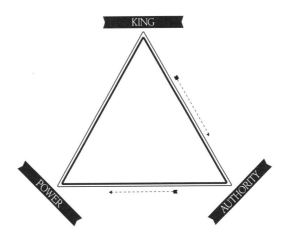

∾ HUDDLE ∾ NOTES

Date ....

What is God saying to me?

....

....

What am I going to do about it?

....

....

....

Date ....

What is God saying to me?

....

....

What am I going to do about it?

....

....

....

Date ....

What is God saying to me?

....

....

What am I going to do about it?

....

....

....

Date ....

What is God saying to me?

....

....

What am I going to do about it?

....

....

....

Date ....

What is God saying to me?

....

....

What am I going to do about it?

....

....

....

Date ....

What is God saying to me?

....

....

What am I going to do about it?

....

....

....

Date ....

What is God saying to me?

....

....

What am I going to do about it?

....

....

....

Date ....

What is God saying to me?

....

....

What am I going to do about it?

....

....

....

Date ....

What is God saying to me?

....

....

What am I going to do about it?

....

....

....

Date ....

What is God saying to me?

....

....

What am I going to do about it?

....

....

....

Date ....

What is God saying to me?

....

....

What am I going to do about it?

....

....

....

Date ....

What is God saying to me?

....

....

What am I going to do about it?

....

....

....

Date ....

What is God saying to me?

....

....

What am I going to do about it?

....

....

....

Date ....

What is God saying to me?

....

....

What am I going to do about it?

....

....

....